AF620033

nineteen

in my raw & vulnerable glory.

@earthenfaerie

I have always wanted to create the kind of book I have always searched so hard for, I admire the raw tender nature of real human experiences and that's what I want to give to you.

This book is not about one particular event, and it's not in any particular order, it's messy because I'm messy, and it's me, at nineteen.

Ebb x

Printed in Australia

I was the warmest place you knew,

and you tried everything you could to make me cold.

My love, you can only smoke so many cigarettes a day, before you start wishing your life away.

You told me that you fell in love with me that
night that in the city,

But I think the purple lights made you blind,

And you fell in love with the idea of me.

She self-destructed

and bought me front row seats.

You told me you hated your eyes
and I couldn't understand why,
There is a whole other universe in them,
And you are the reason I have fallen
in love with the colour brown.

I can see it now,

love in all it's intense,

sticky,

 messy,

 wild,

beautiful glory.

The worst thing you ever did,

was make me start praying,

to a god I didn’t believe in.

She wears red lipstick to make herself feel better,

She wants the boy that called her crazy,

Who taught her, her body wasn't a temple,

She writes it's all my fault, red words, on her mirror,

She's scarred and her teeth chatter but little does she know,

She is temple all on her own,

She wears red lipstick,

And it suits her.

You told me I was too loud and that I cried too much,

But I had to raise my voice to be heard and I only cried because you tried to make me small,

And for a while,

I let you.

You fell in love with an English rose,

Bright brown eyes, and strong, far stronger than you,

The worst thing you ever did was marry her,

For you grew thorns and she began to wilt,

Let her go.

That girl, she is soft spoken, but don't be fooled,
For she a has a light inside,
And it's bigger than both of us combined.

I'm not sure what time it was, and I'm not sure if time even existed that night.

The tea tasted like the earth, but we sipped it anyway and listened to him tell us stories about an old friend, and about the journey he was on.

We giggled at his funny stories and laid back and looked at the stars during his sad ones,

I felt like I was in another universe altogether and it was the most freeing experience I've ever had.

He opened my eyes, she changed my life.

This girl I used to know, she smoked cigarettes out her bedroom window, even when the sun was out.

She couldn't use an oven to save her life, but no one minded.

I usually cooked her dinner on weekends, being friends with her was different to being friends with most people,

She spoke with her eyes.

I don't think she ever saw how much she was.

She didn't think she was much of anything.

But we all knew.

Don't hurt the trees,

The trees know more about you than you do.

Some times abuse isn't just hitting, or yelling,

It's making someone feel small,

It's making someone feel like they are hard to love.

The most important lesson I've learnt in my 19 years,

Is never be blind to things just because you can't see them.

No one is wiser, stronger or braver than the woman who made me.

Perhaps blue moon is just a silly place I made up as kid, but to me it still feels like freedom, like innocence.

Those were the days that I remember, climbing up the trees to my castle, my sister hunting in the woods with her bow and arrow. Those days still feel like home and I hope my children find blue moon one day, and I hope it feels the same for them.

I know you don't know me, but please trust me, the days will get brighter, your heart will get lighter and you'll notice how the moon seems to know your name once again.

My first time was a mess, but the shadows the moon cast across the bed looked pretty, and my second time, she got drunk off a glass of red wine and cried but everything was funny. It used to upset me that my first time wasn't romantic and special, because that's what I thought it was supposed to be, but it was real, and I was clumsy and she spilt wine on me, and honestly, your not supposed to know what your doing. Don't try too hard.

I know far too many girls that have heard their own screams echo out into the night, far too many girls who have fought in their heads for the fear of the consequences of letting "no" escape their lips. Too many girls I know drink too much and too many girls I know feel like their lungs are full of thorns and their bodies are no longer their own.

And far too many boys I know don't care.

I spent far too long wishing I could change things, and far too little time thanking the moon and the stars for things I had.

Even though it was 2am and you were terrified,

you know I would have been on the first plane there.

And held you, whilst you bled.

But you were scared and I understand why,

and perhaps it was a blessing in disguise because the world doesn't need anymore men like him.

Something crazy happened, this universe decided that a girl with messy ponytails, an oversized jumper and hideous yellow gum boots would be the best of friends with a girl with perfect blonde hair and socks that matched her dress.

Since knowing you, I'm slowly but surely falling in love with the sea.

It was a strange time in my life, I forgave things that destroyed me and I picked myself up and rebuilt myself more times than I can count. I broke, I dreamed, I danced, I laughed, I cried harder than I've ever cried, I swore, I smiled but most importantly I loved, and loved hard.

Don't let strangers
write the story of your
life for you.

Even if you don't drink,

go to a bar that's open 24/7, just once.

Dance your heart out all night, and in the morning
go outside and watch the sunrise surrounded by
other people, you don't know,

who are doing the same.

Just once, you won't regret it.

Heartache isn't pretty, it's not fun, it's not romantic, it's not cute. It's hard and it sucks. It is painful. It is quiet and it's loud. It's like a drowning and some days it feels like falling and most days it feels like nothing.

If your heart broken, be heart broken, you don't have to be brave.

Be heart broken.

I don't know if it's the tenderness of soft lips, thighs, or the smoothness of skin. Or the way their eyes widen when you cup their face, their sweet smell, cinnamon and honey, earthy. I think it's all of it, it's all of that and more that I love about women.

Intoxicating.

Magic.

I'd kissed people before.

Many people, many late night drunk kisses,

many kisses with people I thought I knew,

and people I didn't know.

But then I kissed her.

I wish everyone could experience the feeling I got when I kissed her.

Everything I've ever known suddenly seemed like it

had led up to that moment,

And the whole world went quite.

You find peace in the moon, and the moon finds peace in you, and there is nothing more human than that.

You were a fire.
I didn't realise I was being burnt,
until the smoke started to fill my lungs,
and I couldn't breathe anymore.
Suffocated.

You left me for someone else and I still called you, knowing you wouldn't answer, just to hear your voice mail.

And it breaks my heart that someone else is sitting alone doing the exact same thing, trying desperately to hold onto someone who doesn't love them.

I promise you don't need to hear their voice. I promise you don't need to pick up the phone,

You will be okay without them.

It's the most liberating feeling in the world to be okay with being vulnerable.

The fragility of this life never ceases to astound me.

Things change, everything keeps on moving.

Time doesn't stop for anyone.

I was singing a song on a tram and a man in a rainbow coloured suit played along with his ukulele, and a girl with bright blue eyes joined in too. It was such a small thing but I still remember it, I don't think I could ever forget.

My own home doesn't feel like home anymore,

I'm lost in the belly of the beast and I can't breathe.

A labyrinth, a maze, I don't know what to call you,

But I'm so wrapped up and I'm too far gone,

I am in the eye of the hurricane.

I never realised how entirely peaceful the hours after a storm are, I never thought I'd fall in love in the aftermath. Whilst I was picking up the pieces of my life, you simply made sure I knew I had everything in me to start again.

I still hold you,
but in a different way
and
in a different light.

There is no sweet or soft way to put it, you broke my heart, in two.

I swear the whole wide world heard it crack,

it deafened me for so long.

It hurt like hell, and I didn't think it would ever stop hurting.

That's the truth. I didn't think the pain would ever stop.

It's messy and it fucking hurt, there is no use sugar coating it,

your first heart break will take your breath away,

And it will hurt for a long time,

but you will heal.

You will heal.

You will fall in love again, I promise. And then, you'll know what love was always meant to feel like.

You talked about cross roads, like they changed everything,

Like they were a destined path,

Like us meeting was fate.

But I think I was just driving down an old back lane when I broke down,

and on my way home I got lost on a narrow dirt road,

And I couldn't find my way out.

I almost never tried to get back home,

But I'm back now and I still avoid dirt roads.

I had a dream we were walking down the boardwalk in
1981, my girl, with flowers in your hair, white
dress, no shoes, sweet clouds above, soft sunlight.

I had a dream of you last night my love.

It was 1981, along the shore of your hometown,

soft sand, gentle breeze.

It was a time of peace and love for the both of us.

Take me there?

I packed every part I had left of our life in a suitcase,

And I'm scared to open it,

But one day I will,

And I'll burn it.

I kind of miss the sound of glitter clad girls slamming the front gate hard, laughing and clambering up the stairs at 3am.

I secretly kind of loved all of it, beautiful people singing and dancing till the wee hours, cigarettes shared, many stories told.

I've always been an observer, but just watching them be wild, magic, crazy, courageous and utterly themselves, I always felt at home.

I miss that.

I remember the first time, as clear as day,

the first time my body touched yours,

But I cannot for the life of me, remember the last time.

Dance for me,

by the sea,

at sunset,

Dance with me,

by the sea.

It was the

tiny

beautiful

things.

I get so lost in summer, hot sticky days fill me with an unknown angst and frustration, and that stays in me and lingers for months and something about winter, the cold long days and dark skies brings out a peace in me that feels like home.

I am content but long for so much freedom and long for places I have never been.
I am tired, but I am so incredibly awake. I can feel the universe talking to me and telling me stories.
And I'm listening. I'm breathing deeply. And I can feel the ground beneath me, powerful and holy.
I feel her within me.
Sacred.

I write because even during my darkest days,
I turned my pain into poetry,
And it saved me.

www.ingramcontent.com/pod-product-compliance
Ingram Content Group UK Ltd.
Pitfield, Milton Keynes, MK11 3LW, UK
UKHW020231250726
13967UKWH00001B/311

9 780244 487287